A JOU

WITH P.T.S.D.

Scott Blake

chipmunkapublishing

the mental health publisher

empowering people with post traumatic stress disorder

Scott Blake

Published by

Chipmunkapublishing

PO Box 6872

Brentwood

Essex CM13 1ZT

United Kingdom

http://www.chipmunkapublishing.com

Copyright © Scott Blake 2009

Edited by Elaine Evans

Chipmunkapublishing gratefully acknowledges the support of Arts Council England.

ACKNOWLEDGEMENTS

My grateful thanks go to the NHS Mental Health Services for their patience and understanding, to Combat Stress for their support and to my wonderful wife Sara.

A Journey With P.T.S.D.

FOREWORD

This book is an account of my life dealing with a mental illness that was, after several years, diagnosed as Post Traumatic Stress Disorder. It describes the main event that was to severely impede my life for years. There have been changes made to prevent recognition of the specific incident and people involved. It is my intention to depict events and my character, give an insight into the torture that can live with someone and the subconscious way the mind has of dealing with witnessing and participating in tragic events. PTSD is not an illness solely for armed forces personnel in combative action. It can affect anyone at any time when in any dangerous situation that they have seen or taken part in. It can basically be described as an encounter with death. The nature of the traumatic memory does not fade away. It is as if the imprint is so strong that in some people the memory remains as fresh as on the first day.

I cannot praise the fire service fire fighters highly enough. They had their own reasons for striking in 1978 and I am sure it wasn't a decision made lightly. I do not lay the blame at their door. They put their lives on the line every working day. Not knowing what to expect at the next 'shout' or how they would have to deal with it, must be very difficult. Fighting fires and rescuing people, sometimes having to deal with fatalities, must be the ultimate in loyalty to the general public.

I served for only a short period of time as part of a search and rescue team and within that short period I was involved in all kinds of fires with fatalities and rescues, so I understand what it is like to knowingly put one's life in danger in order to save others. I signed up to serve the nation and do so without question.

The following describes one incident and how it was dealt with, and my life after the fire service sorted their differences with the government at the time. It looks at my struggle to deal with my mental illness, PTSD, and learning ways of coping to some degree with it as well as my determination in dealing with everyday problems brought about by PTSD. The actual event has been changed to protect awareness by the surviving family. My suffering with PTSD became severe some 16 years after the events.

It is an illness that is extremely difficult to deal with by oneself. Having support around you from the NHS can help tremendously. I have been extremely fortunate in that I cannot fault the help I had and still do. There are times when my support is increased to help me through the most difficult times.

There are times when I believe my condition is improving but I must never take anything for granted. All it requires is for one of my trigger points to be set off and I am back to square one, suffering terribly.

I never now go into a corner and cry, even when my condition is at its worse, I try to remember that the intensity of my condition will lessen with time and it is with that knowledge that I manage to get through another year. Without support and reassurance I don't believe I would ever have hope of improvement.

Everyone who suffers with PTSD has different experiences but they all have similar component parts. My journey with PTSD may be exclusive to me but I'm sure sufferers who read about my journey will be able to identify with certain parts of it and if they do maybe they will not feel so alone with their problems. Knowing that you are not alone with an illness can, somehow, bring some comfort in an otherwise chaotic world.

It is not only sufferers who may benefit from reading about my journey but also their family and carers, if they are fortunate enough to have them. I hope it will be helpful to them also.

Writing the book was a very difficult exercise for me, bringing back some very severe memories, but with the help of my diaries, I could focus on the good times when I needed to. I shed a few tears but hopefully, they will not have been in vain.

A Journey With P.T.S.D.

Chapter 1

"Don't go in there son, you'll be killed!" shouted the on strike fire officer, but of course, I did and so began my life of torture.

It was a dark, freezing, January night and there was snow on the ground. We had been called out to attend a house fire. The year was 1978 and the fire service was on strike. The armed forces had been put into place to do a job that required a high degree of training and, just as importantly, they always wore flame retardant clothing. Us? Well, we wore combat gear with anti-flash gloves and hoods, pretty useless when wet.

It wasn't the first fire we had been called out to on our period of duty and it wouldn't be the last. But this fire would have far reaching consequences on my life.

On arrival at the scene we were informed there were children trapped in the house and they needed to be saved; there wasn't any argument in my mind, it had to be done. With my breathing apparatus on, I carried a hose pipe up the ladder to the bedroom. The flames were licking me from the ground floor, it looked like an inferno in there, but I couldn't think of that just then, one battle at a time. Struggling with the hosepipe, I managed to climb into the front bedroom. The glass had long since been blown out. Inside the room was thick dense smoke. I waited for my number two to arrive. He didn't look like he fancied the look of this, so I carried on regardless. Saving the children was all that I thought about.

I could see the roof burning fiercely, the timbers plainly exposed and smoke billowing all around them. I lay the hose on what I felt was a bed, it was too difficult to move around the room and search for survivors as well as try and put out the flames. My vision was limited, the smoke intense.

A Journey With P.T.S.D.

Walking around (I walked in a clockwise direction to try to stop myself getting disorientated) there was an obstacle in my way, it was a single bed. Fumbling around the top of the bed I couldn't find anybody in there – so far so good – maybe they had escaped and not been noticed in all the chaos outside – unlikely but I hoped.

Underneath the bed was another matter. There was obviously someone there, curled up in the foetal position. I reached up for the neck and tried to check for a pulse – nothing. I didn't trust the anti-flash gloves I was wearing they were soaked through and pretty useless. I took one off and tried again – no sign of a pulse. Was she dead? (She had long hair), I couldn't risk it, I pulled the body (please don't let her die), out from under the bed. This was going to be very difficult, carrying her down to the waiting ambulance outside. We had never been trained for anything like this but I had to do it. With a tremendous effort she was on my left shoulder – carefully does it – we managed to get down the ladder.

There was screaming from the on looking crowd. I had to block that out, couldn't let my emotions kick in. I lay her down and took my mask off. "There's somebody trapped in the back bedroom – hurry, they are by the window!" shouted someone from the crowd.

I rushed around to the back of the house, guided by some of the men onlookers. Once in the garden I could see things were in a bad way. The fire had taken a major hold, downstairs was totally ablaze and there was flames and smoke billowing out of the upstairs rooms.

"There's a boy up there and a baby!" shouted one of the blokes. "Thanks!" I shouted in reply and once again made my way up a ladder that was being licked by flames from the downstairs rooms.

A Journey With P.T.S.D.

My mask back on, I thought that it would be difficult for anyone to breathe upstairs, the smoke was too thick. Out of nowhere, a young boy appeared with a white bundle of clothes. "Take the baby!" I tucked the small bundle under my left arm and descended the ladder. Once on ground level I gave the baby to the nearest onlooker.

I grabbed hold of the ladder again and looked up; the boy was in the window. "Stay there!" I shouted, but I doubted he would hear me from my mask – everything was muted. Reaching the window, there was no sign of the young boy. I climbed into the room. This was far more serious than the front room. Not only was the room smoke filled but it was very hot, there were flames from the furniture.

I shouted out for the boy – but no response. Fumbling around the room I bumped into a bed, once again I checked it, no sign of him anywhere. My feet were feeling hot – my issue wellingtons may stop my feet getting wet but not much use against heat.

Suddenly I fell, there was a hole in the floor and the flames from below were fierce. I felt trapped. The flames from the burning room were widespread and had latched onto my jacket. The heat from below was fierce but my main concern was falling right through. Thankfully my air bottles were stopping that from happening. I pushed myself up with great difficulty and once out of the hole the flames roared upwards. What should I do?

If the boy was still in the room then he was probably dead but I wasn't going to give in. I tried searching, but was beaten back by flames; there was nothing else for me to do but to withdraw. Something which I was very reluctant to do but my head said it was the only way.

I shouted for the boy one last time, but to no avail. I reluctantly climbed back out of the room and made my way down the ladder. The atmosphere was very solemn amongst the onlookers, they knew as well as I did that the young boy was dead. They didn't blame me but I felt a failure.

I had the chance to rescue him. Why didn't he climb down the ladder after me? I went back around to the front of the house and my team were all looking ashen faced. The girl was dead and so too was the baby.

We stayed around for an hour or two (time seemed of no importance, nothing did) until the fire had burnt itself out with aid of the Green Goddess fire fighters. There was nothing else for us to do but get back to base and wait for the next call out.

The cause of the fire had been a chip pan catching fire in the kitchen. There were two bodies downstairs, the father and the little boy. It didn't help to know that. So many dead. What a waste…

Our search and rescue duty lasted until the end of the strike. We attended numerous fires some with success, some with more fatalities. Who would be a fireman? We were given a week's leave to get over the stint.

I was drunk on the train home and stayed drunk for most of the time. My family were very supportive, not asking about anything, but ready to listen if I talked. Life went on.

Chapter 2

It was never talked about, we were expected to put it behind us and get on with life. I worked hard, but at any opportunity I took to drink. I never thought about why, I just did it.

Months turned quickly into years and the whole thing was forgotten. I left the forces and tried my hand in civvy-street. I was married now and had the responsibility of a house and mortgage. My work took me away periodically, where I would find myself propping up the bar until very late at night. Why? I didn't know. I was either working or drunk. At least I was able to separate the two out from each other.

Over the years my family grew and with that my drinking became less, I had mouths to feed and took my responsibility very seriously. My own childhood had been one long witness to a father and mother constantly at war with each other and I was determined that wouldn't happen with my family.

Promotions through work saw my family and I move south to take on a more responsible roll in management. My drinking stopped but I found myself working longer and longer hours, weekends as well. I saw very little of my young family as they were asleep when I left for work and asleep when I eventually got home late into the evening. This continued until one day on my way to work I had a head on crash, at speed. Fortunately both cars involved were quite big and neither the driver of the other car or I was injured badly. I suffered with whiplash. I went to work the same morning, getting a lift from one of my managers. The warning signs about being a workaholic were there but I ignored them.

It wasn't long before I realised I had a trapped nerve in my shoulder which affected my right arm, physiotherapy didn't seem to work. Fortunately I was in the company health scheme and had manipulation under anaesthetic which cleared it up.

The pressure at work was mounting. We were consolidating our offices and factories, as well as taking over another company. I saw even less of my family.

I managed a weekend off work and went and had an eyesight test, my right eye was giving cause for concern - it had moved to the right and looked pretty odd compared to my left eye. Was this as a result of the crash? Maybe?

I decided to have it corrected and went in for an operation to rectify it. I was home the following day, under orders from the surgeon to take some time off and let it heal properly. I met him halfway and had a fax machine installed in the house. My wife was not impressed. I was just as busy as if being at work. I think she gave up protesting when I had meetings in the house. I just couldn't leave work alone.

It was about a month after the eye operation when things started going wrong. I started having mini blackouts. I went back to my surgeon and he seemed to think it was neurological, nothing to do with the operation. I decided to leave it alone and see what happened over the christmas period, I would go back if the problems persisted.

It was January, 1994 and I had taken my managers out for a drink, in gratitude for all the hard work they had undertaken the previous year. I was on orange juice, a teetotal, and had been since March 1987. Driving home that night I suddenly had a massive pain in my head. I pulled over, opened the door and was physically sick. I got home somehow and continued being sick. I was shaking like a leaf – shock was setting in. My wife immediately called the GP who was very fearful of my condition. I was rushed to hospital. The pain relief they gave me was very welcome but what was the cause? I was given a lumbar puncture.

The next day the doctors' rounds were not very positive. There were traces of blood in my lumbar puncture – a possible bleed from the brain. I was sent to a specialist hospital where more tests were carried out. A subarachnoid haemorrhage was diagnosed after more tests. The pain relief helped but suddenly I thought how vulnerable I was. This couldn't be me? I was in the prime of my life. But it was. Eventually, I was sent to my local hospital from where I was discharged and ordered to stay away from work for a month. They were very firm about this and for once I didn't argue.

During my month sick leave I had what was later described as an epileptic fit and was sent back into hospital. What happened then I can't remember. I can only go on what the doctors and my wife told me. I had a breakdown. I was convinced someone was watching me and whoever it was I was very scared of. I was sent to a mental health clinic for severe cases. I couldn't remember anything. I didn't recognise my family. All that concerned me was the dark figure that followed me around everywhere, whispering something I couldn't quite hear. I was clearly unwell. It was sometime during that period in hospital that I was interviewed by a psychiatrist. I didn't like what was happening to me.

When I was first admitted to hospital, work colleagues would visit me but they tailed off when I was allowed home. The signs from outside of what was going on were that I could be returning to work.

How things changed when I started suffering mentally. It was as if my colleagues believed what I had was contagious, they didn't want to know. They were used to dealing with a strong minded, decision making member of staff not a hollowed out, weak and feeble cry baby who couldn't even look anyone in the eye, let alone stop crying.

I realised a harsh lesson in life, true friends stay around through good and bad times, colleagues only when it is to their advantage. How many true friends had I made? Zero. Life was not only chaotic it was also lonely. My wife did not contact my brothers and sisters. How could she – what would she say?

Things improved slightly and I was sent home. I was visited by a community psychiatric nurse. What was that all about?

Chapter 3

The community psychiatric nurse (CPN), turned out to be a quietly spoken woman, in her thirties. At least I thought she was as I spent the whole of the visit looking down at the floor crying. I don't think she got much out of me in that first session but she said she would come back later in the week.

My home life was a wreck, all I would do was cry and hide in the bedroom curled up in the foetal position under the bed covers. The children were too young to understand and they were frightened by my behaviour. My wife tried to placate them as best she could but the family was under tremendous strain.

The CPN returned. This time I managed to look up a bit but still crying. She asked me what I thought was the matter and all I could reply was that I thought I was out of control, going mad in fact. She was very patient with me and made an appointment to see me soon.

I was starting to have nightmares. There was a man, in the shadows, who kept following me around saying he was going to kill me. My nightmares spread into my daily life. I was in fear of my life. There were times when I couldn't separate out my nightmares from my daily life.

After several visits from the CPN, I eventually managed to string some words together and hold some stilted conversation. She asked me if anything traumatic had ever happened to me – I racked my brain but couldn't think of anything. She asked if I could talk about my life in the armed forces. I would give it a try.

Talking about my early years in the services seemed to relax me slightly as there were some fond memories to look back on – some close friendships. We talked, at length, about my service years when suddenly I remembered my time during the fire service strike. I was completely shocked, I had never even thought about my part in the strike. The fire where the children died came up and instantly things became a lot worse. I found it very difficult to talk about. My nightmares became extremely frightening and throughout the day the memories of that incident became more and more vivid. I was going downhill very quickly.

There were voices coming from somewhere that blamed me for the children's deaths. I started smelling burning flesh, an utterly terrifying smell. My wife couldn't understand what I was going through. The children were frightened of me when I was experiencing these sensations. I was mad; there could be no other explanation. My psychiatrist thought it would be helpful if I went to a day centre for one day per week, to give my wife a break if nothing else but also to give me contact with the outside world.

A Journey With P.T.S.D.

I was terrified of going out of the house. I was even more scared of travelling in a volunteer driver's car to the day centre. For several weeks I couldn't do anything but hide behind a newspaper. I didn't want anyone to see me and I didn't want to see anybody. The voices of the children followed me to the day centre and so too did the smell of burning flesh. I repeatedly asked if anyone else could smell the stench or hear the voices. The staff, like my wife, said they couldn't, there wasn't anything there.

I eventually managed to join in the day centre activities. I painted moulded pottery garden gnomes. It occupied my mind for a while. Looking around the class, eventually, I noticed that the rest of the people there were elderly. I became very upset as I saw no way out of this routine and thought I would be doing this for the rest of my life, which didn't seem too far off. I couldn't bear life.

My CPN continued to come and see me, fitting in around my day centre visits. Time and time again we talked about the fire where the children died. I had become fixated with it.

Family life had become unbearable. I was frightened to be on my own and I couldn't go out, even with my wife. One morning my wife returned from dropping the children off at school and found me searching the bedrooms looking for the figure in the shadows who was shouting at me, blaming me for all that had happened in the fire. It was then that my wife decided she needed help.

It had become evident over the months after my return from hospital and my discussions with the CPN that my short term memory had been severely impaired, possibly as a result of the subarachnoid haemorrhage. I would talk about the same things over and over again. I wasn't making any progress; in fact I was becoming worse.

My CPN arranged for me to go to a specialist hospital to see if they could help. I was absolutely terrified but knew that if I didn't go I would have passed up a chance where some sense of what was happening to me could be found.

It was the most terrifying experience of my life so far. Away from home and surrounded by people who were not very well at all. The patients were mainly suffering with epilepsy which was very upsetting to witness. The days turned into weeks and I eventually became more relaxed in the hospital environment. I decided that I was better and could go home. If only I knew better, things were far from well with me. It was decided that I should go to a different day centre that had an average age group more suitable to me.

My short term memory problems had become more noticeable as time progressed and it was noticed that I found it difficult, impossible, to read and write as well. If I could have gone into a shop I would never have been able to deal with exchanging money.

The new day centre focussed on my literacy and numeracy skills. As for my family, I couldn't see a way out of the situation. My wife and children were finding it more difficult to deal with me. Life was unbearable for all concerned and my wife was finding it too difficult. Her attitude towards me changed and she became intolerant towards me. We started having rows, blame for everything was laid very clearly at my door.

Over the years my condition worsened. My brothers got to know I was ill but were given only slight details. Two of my brothers visited and they were very shocked to see what condition I was in. They did wonderfully well in accepting me as I was and went to great lengths to make me feel as 'normal' as possible. That visit was the death knell for my marriage. As soon as my brothers returned home my wife asked if I had told them how she had been treating me. I hadn't but it made me realise things had to change.

A Journey With P.T.S.D.

I had come from a family where my parents argued incessantly. I was determined that I wouldn't allow my children to grow up in a similar environment. I told my wife that I was leaving, she was extremely upset but I thought she was also relieved. I arranged, or should I say it was arranged for me, to leave home. With a lot of help, I managed it, not only with a mental illness but broken hearted at leaving my children behind.

Chapter 4

I moved into rented accommodation and immediately realised I had not thought things through. I couldn't go out on my own, answer the phone, open letters, answer the door or use the oven. What had I done? Life was very difficult for me; I relied very much on the help from the day centre personnel who were excellent.

It was then when things started to go seriously wrong. I was trapped in a world that I didn't understand and was followed around by voices and smells. I had been seeing a psychiatrist on a regular basis and he prescribed medication for me in larger doses as time went by. They seemed to have some effect but I wasn't sure as things hadn't improved.

At the day centre I was seen by a doctor to try and help me by counselling. The technique he used was very upsetting for me and I always felt worse afterwards and dreaded my next appointment. At the end of each session I was left with the feeling that maybe his technique was part of a grand strategy and that the next time I saw him things would be better for me.

I attended for an appointment one week; feeling apprehensive but needing to see him again; when I was told that he had left the practice unexpectedly and had gone away with the TA for a tour of duty. I was devastated. I immediately asked the staff for help but there was none forthcoming, as he was the only one I would have been able to see. I still had my regular appointments with the consultant psychiatrist but that wasn't for counselling. I felt betrayed by the doctor. I had exposed my inner feelings to him and he had left me without any feeling of closure to the counselling. I was terribly vulnerable to the darker side of my condition and things worsened.

By this time I had been on my own for about six months. My whole world collapsed around me. I was sitting in the living room of my rented accommodation, waiting for transport to take me to the day centre. I heard a voice and looked around. It was the doctor who had tried counselling me. His arm was raised and he was holding my young daughter by her hair and she was screaming for me to help her. I was absolutely terrified. They were as clear to me as if I had looked at my own hand. The doctor shouted at me. "Look here you pathetic scumbag. I have your daughter here. I will kill her if you don't take all your tablets. I'm not joking!"

"OK, OK but please don't hurt her!" I replied, willing to do anything to protect my 5 year old daughter.

I rushed out into the kitchen and opened up my medicine box. There was no question about it I would take the tablets I had left. Within seconds I had swallowed 40 to 50 tablets and rushed back into the living room. He was still there, this time without my daughter.

"What have you done with her?"

A Journey With P.T.S.D.

"She's gone; she's safe, now I want to watch you die."

I then realised I had taken a potentially fatal overdose, I didn't want to die, I wanted to see my family grow up.

I took a chance and ran over to the phone and dialled the day centre. I told the receptionist what had happened and then collapsed on the floor. I was still semi-conscious. If help was going to arrive they would need to get into the house. I struggled to the front door and opened it. I crawled back to the sofa and blacked out.

Chapter 5

Opening my eyes I was confused. I didn't recognise my surroundings and there were things in my throat and nose. What had happened to me? After a while a nurse appeared and explained where I was – in hospital.

Doctors and nurses came and went and eventually the tubes were removed. I couldn't think why I was there, what had I done, had I been in a crash?

A registrar came to see me and told me the story as he knew it. I had taken a very large overdose and was very lucky to be alive. Sitting up in bed confused and frightened my wife arrived.

"Don't think you're coming back home because you've done this!"

I was shocked, how could she say such a thing at such a time?

A Journey With P.T.S.D.

Eventually, I started piecing things together and knew more or less what had happened to me. It took a long time for me to come to terms with it.

I found the general nursing staff very difficult. Because I had mental health problems they dealt with me as if I was a lunatic. Life in the hospital was very difficult. They seemed to think it clever to make fun of me. All the shifts were the same. There was not one person who dealt with me as an ordinary person. I decided to discharge myself. I couldn't take it anymore.

I was admitted to a semi-secure unit for people with mental health problems. The psychiatrist thought it best that I didn't return home until I was feeling better. For the next 18 months I was either in the acute ward or the rehab unit as my demons came and went.

When I was ill, I was severely depressed, anxious and full of guilt. I couldn't get the children's fire out of my head. All I wanted to do was kill myself.

Scott Blake

During this time I was looked after by some excellent mental health nurses, both male and female. To this day I have memories of their kindness, patience and understanding. Once again I was on a lot of medication to help me get through the day and, more importantly, the night.

Eventually I was allowed home to my rented house. I was driven there by a lady I had met at the gym where I used to go with medical staff permission. She was very understanding and supportive, all I could hope for in a person.

We had hit it off during my times at the gym and she was like a breath of fresh air compared to a lot of people I had met. She took me for what I was not for how I was.

Going into the house where I had taken my overdose I immediately felt as though it was a bad place and somewhere I couldn't live without all my problems coming back to me. It was about this time I received a full apology for the day centre's doctor not attending his appointment with me and leaving things very much up in the air. It was of little comfort but hopefully this would never happen to anyone else. Sara found me a flat which I felt safe with.

Once I was settled into life outside hospital I had regular appointments with a psychiatrist who I found it very easy to talk to and he was a very good listener. On one particular appointment he asked me if I had ever heard of Post Traumatic Stress Disorder. I asked him if he meant shell shock and he concurred.

I couldn't be suffering with that, as all my problems originated during peace time. He assured me that PTSD could originate in almost any circumstances. I listened to what he had to say, explaining that the symptoms included depression, anxiety, guilt, flash backs and in some circumstances hallucinations. I couldn't believe what I was hearing, at last I had found a label to package together all my problems – I wasn't mad after all.

Over the following weeks I was informed of all the symptoms and the ways to treat them. A course of sessions with a psychologist was put in place, along with a range of medication to treat the 'package' of PTSD.

The psychologist I met was very understanding and we talked about everything and anything. 'The devil was in the detail' was one of my favourite sayings before I became ill, so we slowly talked about my childhood, my time in the armed forces, working life in civvy street and my family.

A lot of the sessions were very difficult and draining for me but I believed they were a means to an end. There was one major problem whenever I saw the psychologist or psychiatrist, my short term memory was extremely limited and I found it very difficult to remember what had been said. Sometimes I was asked to concentrate on certain aspects of my problem but would soon forget. During this time Sara and I had become very close and she was so important to me and thankfully her feelings were the same. I asked her if she would come to the meetings with me and help me remember what had gone on in the meetings. She agreed without hesitation. She couldn't do enough for me.

As well as being a prompt for me at the meetings Sara researched PTSD and found an organisation called Combat Stress that was for servicemen and women suffering from PTSD. Knowing this made me feel as though I belonged somewhere.

Over the course of a year, it was found that I became worse from October until about mid February. These were very difficult times for me and the symptoms of PTSD returned to almost unbearable limits. My nightmares were extremely distressing, reliving the actions of the children's fire. I could smell the burning flesh and would choke on the smoke, waking up screaming, bathed in sweat.

Throughout the day I would 'see' the children and the doctor (who had tried giving me counselling, which failed terribly – in fact it had compounded the problems). Whenever the doctor appeared the symptoms were severe. The stench of the burning flesh (the boy had been found in the downstairs room, very badly burned), the accusations that I was a coward for getting out of the fire, leaving him behind. The sense of guilt on my behalf was unbearable, no matter how often I was told... I would still regard myself as being guilty for all the deaths.

It was discovered that throughout the day there would be 'triggers' that would set off my suffering. Walking past a burger shop was guaranteed to start my problems off. A log fire burning – bonfire night was dreadful. Watching anything to do with a fire would be another trigger. Sometimes, just seeing a little boy and girl together was enough. It was just part of my life that I had to live with.

As well as the symptom trigger-points, there would be the anniversary dates: starting with the first day of my search and rescue role and then obviously the fire date. I knew this period would pass but when I was living through them all logic would disappear and I would feel as though I was trapped in a time warp that would last forever. In my darkest days I would see no end in sight and self harm and suicide would be in my thoughts for most of the time. I wouldn't believe anyone that the episodes would pass but thankfully they always did. Christmas Day was a day when I would always find myself going into a room somewhere to cry, remembering that the children had had their last Christmas.

Scott Blake

Chapter 6

Sara and I had grown much closer and I had moved into her house, life was on the up for me. Throughout my time away from my children I found it difficult to meet up with them to have some quality time. I was extremely uncomfortable around people and lacked the social skills involved in taking the children out somewhere. They were growing up fast and if I wasn't careful I would miss out on their childhood.

Sara to the rescue, she would pick them up from their house and we would go somewhere 'safe' for me. The children were great they were always protective of me and would look after me if Sara had to disappear somewhere for a few minutes. I look back now and can see how blessed I was with my family. Whenever I was in 'hospital' during the winter months Sara would keep them informed where I was and that I sent my love and would see them as soon as I felt better. Christmas presents were bought in advance.

Not long after moving in with Sara she had a job change. With the distance involved it made more sense to move to a house closer to where she would work.

My care from the NHS would be from a different part of the county. How would I cope with the change? There were lots of questions on my already confused state of mind. It was then that the doctor started being ever present. I was used to him in my nightmares and the occasional visit during the day but now things had stepped up a gear. He was determined that I should kill myself.

During my first winter at our new home I had to go into hospital. There were no familiar faces amongst the staff and the other patients were just as strange. It was a terrible time. I was getting very little sleep and when I did it was full of nightmares. A particular recurring one was my search for the little boy. I was in a smoked filled room that was totally ablaze when, suddenly, I would fall through the hole in the floor and land downstairs. I would land on my feet and be immediately engulfed in flames. I was being incinerated. My mask would melt to my face, I couldn't breathe and I was burning to death. The doctor would be standing in front of me laughing, shouting 'you're dying, you bastard, how does it feel?' I would wake up screaming, choking and covered in sweat. No matter how little sleep I had there was no way I was going to try to get back to sleep again.

I would jump out of bed, brushing myself down as if to extinguish the flames. Eventually I would calm down and realise I was awake and was in hospital with curtains surrounding my bed space. My bed light was already on. I was scared of the dark, too many people lay in the dark, and I needed to see there was no one there when attempting to sleep.

A Journey With P.T.S.D.

After a nightmare I would wander down to the nurses' station and tell them what happened, not the detail, which was for me to suffer. They would be very kind and make me a hot drink. They quickly became aware of my nightly routine and would allow me to go to one of the night-time off-limits rooms to read or watch TV. They knew sleep would not come to me again that night.

The day times would be very difficult as well. The more tired I became, due to lack of sleep, the more visits from the dead children I would get, smelling horribly of burnt flesh, telling me it was all my fault they were dead and they would have their revenge on me. The doctor would appear frequently and when he did I was extremely scared. I was fearful of what he might do to my family.

I was surrounded by patients who were strangers to me and staff, whose trust I wasn't sure of yet. There were daily groups, which I always tried to participate in, hoping that if I kept myself busy I would be less troubled. It had partial success, depending on what the group centred on. I was grateful for small mercies. It was during this time in hospital that I was approached by one of the staff and quietly asked if I heard voices. When I told her I did, it was like a relief valve going off in my head. She told me about a group she ran once a week for people who heard voices and asked if I would like to join in. I jumped at the chance. Anything was worth trying to help with my condition. I was very nervous when the Hearing Voices group was due to be held. I would be in a room of total strangers. What was expected from me? What did I expect from others? The group was quite small, four patients and a member of staff facilitating.

Some of the patients talked in a matter of fact way about the voices they had heard the previous week, whilst others remained quiet until prompted by the facilitator and recounting the previous week was a little more difficult. To my amazement they had all given their voices names and they seemed at home with them. What I was experiencing couldn't be further apart from that.

I managed, very quietly, to speak in front of them. I told them I heard voices from three different people and, depending on who was speaking; they had a greater or lesser effect on me. My voices were aggressive and threatened my life, a long way from the others' voices which seemed orderly. My mind was in chaos. The HV group gave me some very slight relief but it also left me confused, wondering if it was only my voices that were belligerent. I was in fear of my voices and unlike some of the group members; I had no control of them.

During my stay in hospital I became more familiar with the surroundings but due to my poor memory and lack of sleep I found it difficult to get to know the staff or even their names. They were always very busy and appeared, to me anyway, to be short staffed. Staff/patient contact during the day seemed very limited. I felt like I was in a little fortress, being invaded and my defences were starting to crumble. The tiredness was starting to take a strong grip on me. The doctor was terrifying me at night and the dead children were becoming more frequent unwelcome visitors.

After several weeks of going to the HV group I managed to build up the courage and talk about my visits. From the look on the group's faces this was something they had never encountered. I don't think they had heard of PTSD before and the symptoms it carries with it.

Once again I was on my own. I talked to the psychiatrist on a weekly basis whilst on the ward to see how I was getting on and there would usually be a medication change to try and help my condition, especially the lack of sleep. The psychiatrist was very gentle and kind with me, recognising the fact that all was new to me which wasn't helping the way I was feeling. The medication didn't help my sleeping, the nightmares, and the doctor in particular was extremely dominant and things were ramping up. It was the anniversary of the fire in which the children died.

My experiences were horrific: voices, smells, visits by the children and the doctor, all made my condition much worse. I wished I was dead, this suffering was unbearable. During the day I would walk around like a zombie and I would hide in a corner at night time, awaiting the avalanche of hatred to come my way.

Days turned into weeks and soon the frequency of visits and smells would diminish. The voices, I realised, were there to stay. I started managing to cope. I was allowed home for a night at first then gradually I found myself more at home than in hospital. It looked like I had survived my first winter in our new house.

Chapter 7

Whilst I had been in hospital Sara visited me, without fail, on a daily basis, which I was extremely grateful for. She appeared like an oasis of calm in my sea of chaos. When the time was right and she thought I was able to cope around the house she told me she had been in contact with Combat Stress and, if I wanted to, I could go and have a look around, with her, to see if I would like to stay for a few days. This seemed a monumental task but because of her effort I said I would try.

It was a two hour drive to Leatherhead which seemed a very long way. When we arrived we were received very warmly and 'gently' shown around the premises. The first thing I noticed was how relaxed the atmosphere was and how friendly everyone was.

A Journey With P.T.S.D.

The 'patients' were very nice to me, saying how much they enjoyed visiting there and how they benefitted from being surrounded by men who understood what they were going through. They were respected members of the community who made up Combat Stress. I was very impressed with the whole set-up and said so, many times, to Sara whilst I was there.

On the drive back home I said to Sara I thought I would give Combat Stress a try in a few months when I felt more in control of my condition. It was still only the beginning of spring.

An area representative, an ex-officer in the army came and visited me. I had Sara with me for support, telling me a little of what he did, someone I could talk to if I needed to. On his first visit he asked me if I was suffering with depression, shame, guilt, anxiety and anger. When I replied he said that it was very common for the guys at Combat Stress to also be suffering with them. The symptom I didn't have was anger. I felt, once again, more relaxed and assured. I would at least give it a go. The representative was also very well up to date on pensions and asked me if I was claiming any. When I said I wasn't he organised a doctor, experienced in PTSD to come and have 'a chat' with me to see if I qualified for any.

Time passed and one day I received a letter from Leatherhead. I was still unable to communicate with the outside world on my own. Phones, letters and front doors were still off limits to me. It was a letter from Combat Stress inviting me to go to Leatherhead for a week. I was very pleased but also very nervous. I hadn't been away from Sara in years, except in hospital and even then she visited every day.

The journey to Tyrwhitt House seemed to last forever but at the same time was over before I was ready. The staff welcomed Sara and me with a pot of tea for two and a very informal look around the buildings. I had my own room which was spacious

A Journey With P.T.S.D.

and well maintained. Soon it was time for Sara and I to say our goodbyes, this was the first time I could remember being on my own for years. The gates opened in front of the main building and Sara drove out. This was it. All alone, how could I possibly cope? At least I had made it through the gates and decided to stay. I was to learn that it was quite common for sufferers on their first visit to drive right past the entrance and return home, too scared to go in.

I went back to my room and unpacked. I was determined to make the most of my time there so I went to the lounge where some of the men were either reading or playing cards. There was a small library in one of the rooms. I chose a book, at random, and sat down in the lounge area. It took me a little while to settle down, I was very nervous. Before long a trolley with tea cups, tea pots and biscuits appeared, men started helping themselves, I had a go at pouring some tea into a cup but managed to make a bit of a mess, I was too nervous, my hands were shaking.

"Here you go mate, I'll do that for you" one of the guys said as he poured out a cup of tea for me. He introduced himself with a broad grin, putting me at ease. "Is this your first time here?" I replied that it was and he assured me I would settle down in a day or two. It was quite normal to feel the way I was on the first week away from home. The evening went by easier than I thought it would. There was a television room which I went into and found a space to sit. I couldn't get over how friendly everyone was and I certainly felt a lot better by bedtime.

The following morning I was up early and had a shower and dressed when there was a knock on the door. "Good morning, fancy a cup of tea?" I certainly didn't expect that. Luxury!

I was introduced to my key worker who was a lady with an air of calmness about her which immediately reassured me when she looked at me.

A Journey With P.T.S.D.

She told me about the routines and explained that I didn't have to do anything I didn't want to. I was there for my benefit.

There were daily groups that dealt with the aspects of PTSD, I thought I would attend them and see if I could gain more knowledge of the problems I had.

The first group was due to start at 10.00am in one of the TV lounges. I arrived about ten minutes early and found myself on my own. I hoped other people would attend as I didn't fancy a one on one session. By 10.00am there were six or seven of us, once again the guys were friendly and introduced themselves, which put me a bit more at ease. A member of staff appeared and asked if we would like to sit in a semi-circle, which we did. The group was on art therapy. I couldn't draw but the others said they couldn't either. "It's not important how you draw but what you draw. It can be about anything you want. There's no pressure on you to draw things that you will find difficult". We were given some paper and materials to draw with and then started.

My mind went blank, what could I draw? But before I knew it I was drawing a house on fire with people standing at the windows on the inside. I must say that when I looked at it I was pretty uneasy about it. We were invited to talk about our drawings, only if we wanted to. One by one we discussed our drawings and very soon I realised that there was a lot of pain being carried by the guys in the group. I talked about my drawing feeling rather upset about its content. By the end of the group, we all knew each other's names and the problems we were carrying around. There was one unbreakable rule that whatever was discussed in the group was never to be repeated outside of it.

It was quite difficult for me to take in, as after the group we had lunch and I couldn't help looking at the guys in the group thinking about the terrible things they had been witness to. I learned to let go and talk to the guys about everything and before long I had developed a couple of friendships. What was evident was that there was a tremendous amount of mutual respect amongst all the visitors to Combat Stress. Nobody was there without cause.

The days passed quickly. I attended groups that dealt with the constituent parts of PTSD: guilt, shame, anger, depression and with the groups having other sufferers in them, it made me feel easier about myself. I was quite surprised that anger management was discussed as I had never felt anger but I still went to the group to understand what other people were going through.

Before I knew it the week had passed and it was time for Sara to come and pick me up. My key worker, who held one of the sessions every afternoon, asked if I would like to attend again and I said I would. She said she would organise it, once again taking pressure off me, no need to go through the anxiety of knowing if I could attend again etc.

Whilst I was at Tyrwhitt House I met the consultant psychiatrist and he put me at ease about my condition, telling me I had all the classic symptoms and he would write a letter to my psychiatrist at home, suggesting some medication which he had found useful for other sufferers.

Sara arrived and it was time to go home. I said my farewells and returned home. I felt, for probably the first time in many years that I wasn't alone with my illness. That itself made me feel more positive about myself.

It was during my positive times that I decided to do some volunteer work. I asked my old teacher, from my day centre days, if I could help out in any way. He was a horticulture instructor. We discussed what would be best for me and agreed what days I could help.

There was one major problem in volunteering and that was, how would I get there? I was afraid of being on my own and had no transport of my own.

A Journey With P.T.S.D.

My key worker helped me with my confidence and I gradually built up to being able to catch the bus to outside the college where I would do my voluntary work. I helped out with a class of youngsters with learning difficulties, which I found very rewarding and soon felt I was part of the team helping them.

Chapter 8

When winter came around things started going wrong for me. Throughout the year I had still been experiencing hearing voices and having nightmares (although the nightmares were less severe and I could return to bed and go back to sleep). The awful smells would come back whenever I smelt hamburger shops etc and also in the winter when wood fires were burning in people's houses. I found it more and more difficult to do things on my own. The doctor would appear at the bus stop, preventing me getting on, telling me the bus would crash and I would die. The children and the doctor together would appear more frequently shaking me to my roots. I would lose all rationality when I was in the presence of them.

My CPN visited me on a weekly basis and did her best to assure me that what I was seeing wasn't real. I tried to understand and agree but when I was having a 'visit' it was as real as if someone was in the room with me. I became ill again. The doctor and the children tried convincing me that I should kill myself and if I didn't the devil would come and kill Sara. When I managed to resist killing myself (I planned how I would do it, over and over again) the doctor said Sara was the devil and that I should kill her. It was then that my CPN advised me that a stay in hospital would be best for me.

My poor memory was a hindrance. I couldn't remember being on the ward previously and as a consequence I felt very vulnerable, not only from my demons but from other patients. Now I was back in the cycle of events that felt like a curse: The winter months.

Life was very difficult and things got a lot worse before they got better. The anniversary dates were particularly bad, during these periods I felt as though all hope had gone and I couldn't see a way out other than killing myself. The ward-staff were friendly and reassuring to me and the psychiatrist managed to help me get some sleep, but I still felt unbearably tired and run down.

After a while, the anniversary had passed, things started becoming clearer to me and the children and doctor had less effect on me. Soon it was time for me to go home again. I had survived another year.

Sara and I went on holiday in February as a celebration of the passing of the bad times. We went abroad and I felt anonymous amongst the locals, no one knew me. I felt a lot safer. We soon realised that a holiday in February was a great idea. It would give me something to look forward to and it would be a sign of the bad times passing. We made this an annual event.

My friend who taught horticulture was very welcoming when I said I thought I could return to helping him. The students were pleased to see me back. Life became easier.

A Journey With P.T.S.D.

As I only did volunteer work a couple of days a week I had days off in which I would go to a weekly Hearing Voices group; my attendance would fluctuate with my illness condition. My psychiatrist asked me if I would like to go and see a psychologist to help me with my condition. There was a waiting list but due to my poor memory I forgot all about it, so when a letter arrived telling me I had an appointment it seemed as though I had been waiting no time at all.

The consultant psychologist made me immediately feel at ease with him. I was going to have Cognitive Behaviour Therapy (CBT). The sessions were weekly and lasted an hour. My poor memory got in the way to start with so he would write me notes telling me if I had any 'homework' (things to work on during the week). Some of the suggestions worked, some didn't. One particular coping strategy I found to be successful was the use of imaginary spirals. Whenever I was suffering in any way, with smells, voices, or visits, I could use the spiral technique which involved imagining two spirals rotating (in opposite direction to each other). Wherever my problem was, stress across my shoulders for example, I would concentrate on bringing the spirals together across my shoulders – the spirals could take on any dimension – and the pain would go away: Wonderful.

From time to time my condition would worsen, surprisingly sometimes through the summer months and it would be such that I would be asked if I wanted to go into hospital.   I was determined not to.   I used all my coping strategies that I had learnt and they lessened the effect of my experiences.

My memory was causing concern with the psychologist and he referred me to a neurological psychologist at the General Hospital. After a series of visits and more tests it was revealed that my memory was, in fact, impaired. I was also lacking in hand/eye coordination and my processing skills were very limited. Now I knew for sure what I had believed. It was of little comfort to me but at least it was another test out of the way.

Chapter 9

During the previous 12 months, whilst seeing both a psychologist and a psychiatrist there were changes within the NHS. I would still see my CPN on a regular basis but I was introduced to someone from a CMHT (Community Mental Health Team) who would provide me with support by taking me out for one hour per week. This was of great benefit to me as I was house bound unless Sara was not working. I had to give up my volunteer work as I found it too stressful. One hour per week didn't sound like much but I really looked forward to it.

A change of scenery was certainly most welcome. I found it difficult to build up trust with the community support worker. It may have been a personality clash, who knows, you cannot get on with everyone in life, but I was still very grateful for the support. As well as going out one hour per week I was to see an art therapist, having been referred by the psychologist.

Art therapy was something I had attended at Combat Stress and although quite painful it was an opportunity to externalise my nightmares and visits. What I didn't realise was that the art therapy sessions were one on one; there was no group, nowhere to hide. The therapist was very kind and took things at my pace. I was never under any pressure to do any drawing; I could just talk if I wanted to. I decided I would draw a picture. Once again the image of the burning house came out, along with the burning bodies. I became very distressed but the therapist recognised this and we talked things through and I went away from the session feeling quite drained but relieved that I had attended.

The following week took up the same routine, but instead of drawing the house with the children in, I drew something completely different. It suddenly occurred to me that there were several fires I

Scott Blake

attended where there were fatalities but I had 'forgotten' all about them. I felt quite disturbed by this and worried. Would I have the same problems from the person dying in the picture I had drawn? Only time would tell. Throughout the week I was plagued by thoughts and images of the second fire I had drawn. The children and doctor were making my life unbearable. They now had further proof, according to them, that I was a coward and had let people die, when I could have rescued them.

I became very upset but decided it best to continue with the art therapy and see if things got any better. The next session brought out another drawing, more fatalities, where had they been hiding? Life became very difficult but I never had visits from the other fatalities. After two more weeks and the further exposure to two more fires, I decided that it was probably in my best interest if I stopped going to art therapy. The therapist was very understanding and so too was the psychologist, at least I had given it a try.

A Journey With P.T.S.D.

Over the following weeks, thoughts about the other fires diminished and the visits from the children and doctor concentrated themselves on what had happened to them.

Winter was soon upon me again and my problems moved up a few gears. I was determined I would deal with my problems without going into hospital. My CPN, psychiatrist and psychologist combined to make my life easier for me. Dealing with my symptoms as a team, using aversion and coping strategies, as well as the opportunity to talk more often about what was happening to me. It was extremely difficult but I managed to avoid going into hospital.

I still had feelings of guilt and shame, as well as being afraid of what was happening to me, but felt part of a team helping me through my darkest days. Sara was wonderfully supportive. When January turned into February and the holiday we had planned had come around, I felt for the first time in many years proud of my achievement. I believed that if I coped, along with a tremendous amount of support from the health care team, I would get through the year with fewer problems.

'Visits' from the children, accompanied by their horrible smell remained constant and when I was feeling particularly low the doctor would arrive to make things even worse and order me to kill myself. It was only through great determination and referring back to my diary that I managed to get through. I had been keeping a daily diary for years to enable me to look back at the good days. Good days did exist, reading my diary backed that up.

Over the next 12 months I tried to stretch myself by doing things that previously I would have thought impossible. I was able to use the telephone, as long as I called the number I felt in control. I still felt unable to answer the phone, fearful of who may be calling. I became more able to answer the front door, as long as I could see who was there by looking through the window. If it was an unexpected call I couldn't manage to do it, once again fearful of who may be calling.

I accompanied Sara to the shops and as long as I had her to hold on to, or a shopping trolley, it was easier. I soon found out which shops I could go in without hearing voices. One thing at a time. I avoided the noisy supermarkets, they would be for later.

It was soon realised by everyone that as long as I was sticking to the routine that I had built up, with the help of Sara, I could manage to get through the day. If I was to break the routine, for whatever reason, things became very difficult for me. It was decided, by all, that small steps forward was the best way to progress. If I operated within my safety zone, then I could manage my routine. Any change in routine would shake me up and my symptoms would sometimes be too difficult to manage.

I had another visit to Combat Stress in Leatherhead which once again I found difficult at first. Being so far away from Sara was very stressful for me. Everyone at Combat Stress was very friendly and supportive and once I had settled in I began enjoying the experience. It was very difficult for me to book time away from Sara but once away I felt secure at Combat Stress, surrounded by men who had mutual respect for each other.

Throughout all that had been happening to me over the years I must say that having the love and support of my children; who were quickly growing up; and Sara was of great comfort to me and helped enormously in dealing with my day to day life. Without that love and support my life would have been unbearable, but I was very fortunate. Sara would organise get-togethers with the children and we would have a great time going out for a meal or playing some type of game. I made great efforts to appear 'normal' when out with them. But sometimes my facade slipped and the family were

A Journey With P.T.S.D.

there to help me. They understood that I sometimes had very bad times and it was probably not best to meet up. The children have never asked what is wrong with me they just accept me as I am, their father.

During my years of being unwell and then being diagnosed as having PTSD, I have been very lucky with the care and support I have had from psychiatrists, psychologists, therapists, nursing staff and support workers. I have always found that being honest and polite has led me to having positive feedback. I understand that facilities differ throughout the country and some mental health care centres are under greater pressure than others. But once 'in the system' the care involved is first rate and a tribute to the NHS. There have been many changes in the structure of the NHS. One of the main changes that effected me was the closing of the day centres in the area that I live. It gave me a sense of purpose for the day. Getting out of bed and being ready for the transport to take me to the day centre, even through my most difficult days when I thought I was going mad, making an effort to have some structure to the day helped.

I understand that not everyone is as fortunate as I have been. But having had the various services available to help me through the day, in preparation for the night ahead, I hope others will 'stick with it' and see what develops. Once in the system I am sure, if my experiences are anything to go by, help will be at hand.

PTSD is a difficult illness to diagnose as it comprises of several problems each of which can make a person mentally unwell. Anxiety; depression; guilt; anger; fear of contact with the outside world; terrible nightmares and feelings of hopelessness because you feel on your own and no one understands, not even yourself, what is going on inside your head; hallucinations and smells can be a daily battle that can wear the sufferer down. The nightmares become exhausting and compound the problems because of the lack of sleep.

Because of the conflicts the country has been involved in, the number of people suffering with PTSD has increased and resources are becoming more stretched. But PTSD is now a recognised illness and hope and help are attainable. Anyone can suffer with PTSD who has been involved in or witnessed some traumatic event. It is not a weakness to suffer with PTSD it is just a fact of life. It is not only people from the armed forces who are exposed to the trauma leading to PTSD, ambulance crews can be just as easily. They deal with traumatic events every day of their working lives.

During the First World War it was called 'shell shock', similarly in the Second World War. It was investigated during the Vietnam War, with American soldiers returning from combat and going straight into 'normal' everyday lives. Trying to bridge the gap between being in battle and hours later in civvy street can have a tremendously harming effect on the ex-service personnel.

Combat Stress in Leatherhead do a fantastic job in receiving sufferers and helping them to come to terms with their experiences and more importantly, in my view, having a sense of belonging. Spending some time with sufferers of PTSD helps enormously. The groups that are run daily help you understand the component parts of PTSD and how you can deal with them. Although I found the groups difficult it was a relief to externalise my feelings and thoughts that had been bottled up for years. It is not a cure but it allowed me to manage my problems. I still have PTSD and I still have bad times in the winter months but I try very hard to get on with a normal life within my own safe boundaries. It is not perfect by any means but when I look through my old diaries I can see I have progressed, only slightly maybe, but nevertheless there has been some improvement.

A Journey With P.T.S.D.

Chapter 10

Writing this journey with PTSD has been an emotional experience with memories coming back that I would rather have avoided but if only one person takes inspiration from what the story holds then it will have been worth the effort.

At my time of writing it is in the 'Good Months', long days and short nights. I am still 'visited', still hear voices and experience the smells but I know in time they will pass. Logic is with me when I'm in the 'Good Months'. I am in the first part of trying to establish a meeting group for PTSD sufferers, hoping that meeting up will help. It will not be a war story group but will concentrate on dealing with the everyday problems the illness throws up and, if necessary, putting people in contact with helpful associations. Maybe by dealing with the component parts of the illness, the intensity of

PTSD will be reduced to a manageable level. Also having social contact can be of enormous benefit.

Not everyone with PTSD has heard of Combat Stress and the fantastic work they do. It may be possible to be referred there. Having hope and the feeling of belonging for me has changed my life, in small steps, but nevertheless there has been improvement. If it can happen for me then it could be possible for someone else. There are people in the NHS who are there to help, as they have with me, in lesser or greater degrees but what is important to hold onto is that PTSD is now becoming more recognised and help is at hand.

I know that taking that first step is the most difficult one but having the courage to do so, with help if necessary, can improve a sufferer's quality of life. Talking to someone about your problems can be like a relief valve. Do not store up your problems, externalise them and let those who can help you, understand how you are feeling.

A Journey With P.T.S.D.

Thirty years ago, as far as I know, there was no such thing as a debrief after involvement in traumatic events, in fact it was the opposite, people were expected to 'get on with it', 'pull your socks up' and get on with the next job. I wasn't involved in combat action just doing a fireman's job and it affected me, without realising, for the rest of my life. Now, I don't regard myself as being weak for suffering with PTSD but unfortunate. It can lay unrecognised for years, as it did with me. I covered over the cracks by drinking very heavily (I didn't know why then) and becoming a workaholic in civilian life, until my body told me to stop. It is important to talk and with that talk recognise the problems and finally identify the suffering of PTSD.

There is hope, I have it and I never thought it would be possible to improve my condition but I have, albeit slightly, but I have a sense of peacefulness at times that are worth the bad times. The longer I have peacefulness the greater the hope that one day I might go through a winter without my

Scott Blake

problems. Once you have that hope, keep hold of it
and don't let go of it and things could get better.

Printed in the United Kingdom by
Lightning Source UK Ltd., Milton Keynes
139291UK00001B/32/P